Northern Nib

A Bit of Skull

and other Barmy Ballads from Ireland!

Poetry by Robert E. Wilson
Illustrations by Kathryn Bannister

Contents

Introduction

Here's a second batch of bizarre ballads conceived and created in Ireland! Like my first collection, 'The Cullybackey Counterfeiters...' it's another crazy cocktail of original ideas, true happenings and anecdotal tales ('old yarns') I've gathered up over the years!

As with my earlier work, the aim of this collection is to provide a bit of light reading through the medium of narrative verse (and some pieces, I'm sure, can be read as performance poetry).

You'll notice there's a brief introduction to each piece, sometimes explaining how it came to be written. I'm eager to encourage others to write and I hope this helps show how an idea that sounds almost believable on the one hand and absolute blether on the other can provide inspiration for creative writing!

Once again, I'd like to thank a few people for their support and encouragement. Author and poet Lynda Tavakoli, the resourceful tutor of our writers' group, literary agent Bill Jeffrey for his wise counsel and all my fellow writers for their support and good wishes. I'm also delighted to thank artist Kathryn Bannister for the original illustrations she has produced for this book.

Now sit back and enjoy a bit of blarney!

Robert E. Wilson, October 2016.

About the Author and Artist:

Robert E. Wilson is from County Antrim, Northern Ireland. An active member of an established writers' group, he contributed to the 'Linen Poetry and Prose Anthology' published in partnership with the Irish Linen Centre, Lisburn, which is available on Kindle. He is a regular reader at the 'Purely Poetry' evenings in the Crescent Arts Centre, Belfast, has participated in the Bard of Armagh Festival of Humorous Verse and was a finalist in the Connemara Mussel Festival Poetry Competition 2016, judged by the esteemed Irish poet Eamon Grennan.

Robert's first collection of humorous poems, 'The Cullybackey Counterfeiters and other Barmy Ballads from Ireland' is available on Amazon.

For further information on Robert's work, visit his website: www.northernnib.weebly.com or follow on Twitter @WilsonNib

Kathryn Bannister is an artist and illustrator from Northern Ireland. She graduated from Ulster University with a Degree in Fine and Applied Arts.
Kathryn can be contacted at instagram.com/kathrynbannisterart or on facebook.com/inkberrydesign

A Bit of Skullduggery

a marketing tale...

My first offering in this collection is a ballad inspired by a lot of 'oul blether' – an anecdote I once heard about a man trying to sell skulls to tourists near Dublin Airport. I'm sure it wasn't true, but as for **this** tale?

Russell P. Zukowski, from Cookeville, Tennessee
Flew in to Dublin Airport, his Irish roots to see;
Quite recently retired from work and worth a right few dollars,
He thought he'd visit Erin's Isle, the land of saints and scholars.

He rented a convertible and didn't stop or stay
Till ending up in Ballyfree, upon its market day;
Russ noticed that this village lay upon the tourist route
And parked just off the main street, to mosey round on foot.

He thought he'd browse the stalls awhile to see what there might be
As gifts for all the folk back home in Cookeville, Tennessee;
There was hustle and some bustle, interspersed with quiet lulls
When suddenly, Russ saw a stall laid out with – *human skulls!*

He looked again in disbelief and puzzled at the sight
Of wooden shelves bedecked with skulls, across from left to right;
A stout, congenial man stood there, who beckoned him to come:
'Good morning, sir, I'm Duggie. Tell me, where might you be from?'

'I'm all the way from Cookeville, in the state of Tennessee,'
Said Russ, 'and now, about these skulls, I'm curious as can be;
Am I to take it that you're selling *skulls* to passers-by?
I've never seen the like before and, man, that ain't no lie!'

'Well, sir,' said Duggie, 'glad you asked a question of that kind –
Each skull you see before you is a great historic find;
They're not just bones and teeth from some old unmarked burial site,
But relics of our noble dead, displayed in broad daylight!

They're skulls of famous Irishmen and women through the age,
Of warrior and poet, of scholar and of sage;
Take this one, for example, sir, a simple skull to you,
But it belonged to our great ancient hero, Brian Boru.

And see this skull, sir, at the front, the second one along?
The girl that it belonged to is immortalised in song;
From Dublin city and so pretty – sweet Moll-ee Malone,
And here's the skull of patriot leader, Theobald Wolfe Tone.

But *this* one, at the back, sir, is the greatest skull of all,
It *would* look quite in place, I'm sure, in some grand lecture hall;
And *do* you know, sir, *why* I've placed it on the *topmost* shelf?
It's that of none more honoured than our *Patron Saint* himself!'

'You mean you've got *St Patrick's* skull?' Russ gasped in disbelief!
'Hey, tell me, man, what are you now, some kind of graveyard thief?
If that's Saint Patrick's skull, it must be sixteen centuries old –
You've brought it to a *market place* to get the darn thing sold?'

'Don't be alarmed, sir,' Duggie smiled, 'I'm nothin' o' the kind;
I've told you every skull here is a true authentic find!
My nephew Sean unearths the likes of helmets, bones and rings;
He's an arch–e-ol-o, ach, you know – a man who digs for things!'

'I guess I might be getting old but, man, a fool I ain't,'
Said Russ. 'I see great value in the skull of Ireland's Saint;
Why, I'm prepared to buy it, if you'll tell me what it's worth –
Saint Patrick's skull must be among the greatest finds on earth!'

He smiled, 'Five hundred Euro and the skull is yours to keep;
Just work it out in dollars, sir – I don't think that's too steep.'
'Consider it a deal,' said Russ. 'How thrilled they're gonna be
When I show *this* to folk back home in Cookeville, Tennessee!'

Well, two years passed and Russell P. Zokowski came again
To Dublin Airport in a similar transatlantic plane;
He rented that convertible (it cost him slightly more)
And ended up in Ballyfree, just like he'd done before.

Russ headed to the market and meandered round each stall,
Then stopped with mouth wide open and he looked about to fall,
For there, as if he'd never moved and in the same old place,
Was Duggie with his skulls again, a smile upon his face!

Well, Russ approached without delay: 'Hi man, remember me?
It's Russell P. Zokowski here, from Cookeville, Tennessee.
Are you still selling skulls? Why, man, oh, man, I mean to say –
I'm every bit as curious now! So, who've you got today?'

'Now, sir,' said Duggie, 'This one's new, but I'm sure it will sell,
The skull of that great Irish statesman, Charles Stewart Parnell;
And see this skull? My nephew found it buried in a cave
High up a hill in Sligo – it belonged to fair Queen Maeve.

Here's the skull of Michael Collins, a champion of Home Rule,
And this *huge* skull was once the head of giant Finn MacCool,
But I've one that's *very* special and that's why I placed it there,
Upon the *top* shelf, sir, for it's *Saint Patrick's* skull, I swear!'

'Hey, hold on, buddy,' Russell said, 'the last time I came here
I bought Saint Patrick's skull from you and, man, it cost me dear!
I paid five hundred of your notes and now you're tellin' me
That *this* skull is St Patrick's, not my one in Tennessee!'

'Sure, don't you worry,' Duggie said, 'there has been no mistake;
I'm an honest man, believe me – not one skull here is a fake!
'Twas *old* Saint Patrick's skull you bought – that last one that I had;
This one's the skull of *young* Saint Pat, when he was just a lad!'

Woolly War of Words

a farming tale...

A *story about two old characters who'd argue that black is white or, in this case, over the colour blue!*

Oul Wullie John McAllister,

A farmer in the Glens,

Bought a wheen o' Galway sheep

And stuck them in two pens

To mark them, then he turned them loose

Upon the hillside free;

With blue paint sprayed on every one,

His flock was plain to see.

Oul Wullie had a neighbour, now,

A farmer called O'Neill;

He'd known oul Danny fifty years

And barely could conceal

The fact that he detested him,

There were no 'ifs' or 'buts' –

They both seemed destined, since their youth

To hate each other's guts.

Then what made things wild difficult

For our oul Wullie John

Was, twenty-somethin' years ago

His daughter, wee Siobhan

Had married Danny's son, big Hugh

And that just made things worse –

Now every family gathering

Became to him a curse!

So, this day they were bellowin'

Like two force seven gales

About a flock of Mountain Sheep

Oul Danny got from Wales.

'What's wrong wi' ye?' snapped Wullie John,

'Ye sent yon gulpin, Hugh

To put a mark upon them, an'

He's gone an' done them *blue!'*

'Ach, dry ye'er eyes!' O'Neill replied,

'An' go an' boil ye'er heed –

What stopped ye markin' *yours*

Some ither colour – green or reed?'

'I did mine first,' growled Wullie John,

'An then, I just suppose

You marked your sheep the same as mine

So you'd get up my nose!'

O'Neill drew breath then guldered,

'Ach, shut up – I'll hear no more!

I bought that paint at discount price

From Billy Mackey's store.'

'Well, so did I,' said Wullie John,

'But, couldna' even you

Have picked a colour for your sheep

That wasna' like mine – *blue?*'

'It was the only colour left,'

Said Danny, 'in his cart.'

Then Wullie John snapped, 'How will locals

Tell our sheep apart?

If my yins wander down the lane

Or in some hedge get stuck,

And if yon stupid ram o' yours

Falls headlong in a sheugh?'

The two oul boys kept quarrellin',

(Ach, most was Double-Dutch!)

Said Wullie John, 'Ye make a hames

Of *everything* ye touch!

It hardly would surprise me

If ye got yon eejit, Hugh

To spray a blue mark on *your* heed

So *your* sheep know it's *you!*'

Well, the two o' them got madder,

Both got louder, both got thran;

You'd have heard them in Glentaisie,

You'd have heard them in Glenaan!

But, standing there, between them,

And as quiet as could be

Was Siobhan and Hugh's young daughter,

Aged six – wee Ann Marie!

Now, the pair o' them went silent

As she tugged on both their coats

And, suddenly, inside they felt

Like two oul mountain goats;

'Grandad Danny, Grandad Wullie John,'

She said, 'What's your complaint?

Why *are* you fightin' over some

Old silly pot of paint?

You *really* think that no-one here

Can tell your sheep apart?

Ach, Grandads, it's so easy,

I could do it from the start!

Grandad Danny, all your sheep are *black,*

So why this silly fight?

Sure all yours, Grandad Wullie John,

From head to tail are *white!'*

A Most Musical Medical Mystery

a tale that hits all the wrong notes...

I 'composed' this ballad about a Belfast man of 'note' who takes a wee bit of deception to a new 'scale'!

Dan Kearney lived in Belfast, down in Ponderosa Street,
Ach, everybody knew him as 'Wee Dan';
A more easy-going 'crater' you would scarcely ever meet,
He's what the folk there called, 'a brave wee man'.

Now, in spite of all his virtues, wee Dan had just one big vice –
No matter where you'd bring him, near or far,
You'd only have to turn away or blink just once or twice
To find him in the nearest public bar.

Sure, he hardly made it home some nights from work, without a stop
At 'The Foxhound' or 'The Fiddler' on the route;
Sometimes he'd down a wee quick pint, then on the bus he'd hop
Or eventually just stagger home on foot.

Well, one day, Dan's wife Mary said, 'Dear, don't you think it's time
That you put up thon kitchen shelf for me?
In fact, there are a few wee household jobs you know that I'm
Quite keen that you'd get finished before tea.'

'Ach, Mary, I'd just *love* to help, but I've got kinda slow;
The truth is, that I'm never feelin' great,'
Said Dan. 'It's likely just my *age* that's startin' now to show –
I'm not thon young lad that you used to date!'

That frown appeared on Mary's face – one Dan knew *very* well,
'I know fine rightly where your problem lies,
And so do you, Dan Kearney – ach, I shouldn't have to spell
It out to you again – it's no surprise..

..At all,' she said, so crossly, 'that you're never feelin' good
And lie all weekend snorin' in your bed;
You spend more time in public bars you know you ever should –
It's no wonder that you can't lift up your head!

But, if this is like *all other weekends* – let me get it right –
Though you've been feeling poorly for six hours,
You'll suddenly be well enough by eight o'clock tonight
To head down to the "The Fiddler" for some jars!

So, just you go this Monday, Dan and see thon Doctor Hughes,
Though he'll just tell you what we all are thinkin' –
The only thing that's wrong with you is shiftin' too much booze
And what you need to do is quit the drinkin'!'

Well, on Monday Dan put on his coat and headed off to see
The doctor, just to put all this to rest,
Who checked him up and told him, 'You're as well as you can be,
But your lifestyle is not possibly the best.

As your doctor, Mr Kearney, I'm concerned that you consume
More alcohol than you should really drink;
Although you're healthy at the moment, please do not assume
That it's okay – so cut back, don't you think?'

That posed a problem for wee Dan; the doctor's diagnosis,
Whatever way he tried to dress it up,
Was word for word exactly as predicted by his missus
And, there'd be absolutely no let-up..

..In Mary's bargin', once she knew what Doctor Hughes had said,
So Dan thought, 'To the *library* I'll go
And invent a diagnosis from an article I've read –
Some clever word that Mary just won't know!'

Well, in the 'Music' section wee Dan opened up a book
At random and thought, '*That* defies translation;
Mary won't have heard *this* term, she'll not know where to look –
Yep, there's the word I'll use: it's *syncopation!'*

So, with the strange word *syncopation* whizzing round his mind,
The cure for this he started now to think,
Was rest at home, attended by a wife that's good and kind
And, medicinally, to have the odd wee drink!

'Now, let me see, dear: what might Dr Hughes have said to you?'
Asked Mary, once wee Dan stepped in the door;
'Well, Mr Kearney, glad to say you're lookin' good as new,
But, I'm tellin' you, you mustn't booze no more?'

Wee Dan smiled back so smugly, 'He said nothin' of the sort,
But concluded, after serious consultation
With his colleague Doctor Morgan, he was sorry to report
That I've a chronic case of *syncopation!*

Now, dear, please fetch my slippers and I'd love a cup of tea;
I can't do much unless it's very light.
I'm told, in my condition, that a *rest* is good for me,
But it's okay if I have a drink tonight.'

Well, Wee Dan mentioned *syncopation* every day that week,
Each time he felt some job was 'cryin' out',
Though it never stopped him in the evening from a quiet sneak
Down to the pub, to have a glass of stout!

Now this left Mary baffled but quite curious, all the same,
For no-one that she spoke to round the town
Had ever heard of any ailment going by this name
And, on a scrap of paper, wrote it down.

Then she made it her life's mission to discover what it meant,
But even Jane, her nurse friend hadn't heard
Of this term *syncopation* and the woes it might foment,
Or any ailment sounding like that word.

Now, *Friday* came and wee Dan said, 'The weekend is in sight,
I'll play the "syncopation card" again,
For it's workin' well with Mary, so when I come home tonight
It won't be hard to all those symptoms feign.

But, as soon as Dan walked in the door, wee Mary greeted him
With twenty jobs she'd written on a list,
Which she proceeded then to read in accent harsh and grim
And finished with, 'Now is there one I've missed?'

'Ach, what's the matter, Mary?' asked wee Dan in disbelief.
'Have you forgotten I've got *syncopation*?'
'I'll tell you what's the matter,' Mary answered. 'I'll be brief,
All week I've made it my preoccupation..

..To find out more about this ailment no-one's ever seen
And the facts behind the doctor's diagnosis,
But now that I've discovered just what "syncopation" *means,*
I agree in full with Doctor Hughes' prognosis!

You thought when you said, "syncopation" I'd not know a thing,
But you were wrong to take me for a fool,
For today down in the Co-Op I ran into Annie King,
The music teacher from our daughter's school.

Well, Annie stood and gave to me the clearest explanation
And I now see that your strange ailment's true
And, I know that if *anyone* round here has *syncopation*,
Dan Kearney, dear, the classic case is *you!*

For, when I said you'd *syncopation*, Annie split her sides,
"That term is used in *music!* How bizarre!"
She told me that its meaning can be simply summarized:
"To move unsteadily from bar to bar!"'

Dear Santa...

a Christmas tale...

Another Belfast tale, inspired in part by a real-life incident with a little bit of blarney thrown into the mix!

With just three days to Christmas, the Belfast Royal Mail
At nineteen to the dozen, was striving not to fail
To get all cards delivered, those parcels to the door,
And nowhere was more busy than the Sorting Office floor.

The section marked 'Lost Letters' was working hard to cope
With an incomplete address on the occasional envelope;
Maggie Flynn was at her desk there when a letter came her way
Addressed to 'Santa, Snowland' – the most curious one that day!

Now, in such a situation, like all staff, Maggie knew
To open up the letter and try to find a clue
As to the place it's going, or the route it might have come
And, right away, she quickly found where this strange note was from.

It said, '25 Glenveigh Street' and, in a shaky hand,
Was scrawled a simple letter that a child might understand;
It started off, 'Dear Santa' and, though private it should stay,
Our Mags could not resist the urge to read it anyway.

'I'm eighty-seven years of age, my family's far away,
I'm all alone and freezing as I can't afford to pay
To heat my home this Christmas so, if some cash you can spare,
About a hundred pounds or more would be a treat most rare.'

She signed it 'Betty Harper' and her letter tugged a string
Inside young Maggie's kindly heart, who felt that she should bring
This note to show her office pals and have a quick whip round
To see if what was needed for old Betty could be found.

Now, the staff in Maggie's sorting room were able just to cough
Right up the sum of ninety pounds, which Maggie then sent off
To Betty in the final post, as she left work that day,
To make sure that their secret gift arrived without delay.

Well, Christmas came and Christmas went and, back at work again,
Our Maggie saw an envelope addressed in Betty's pen
To Santa Claus in Snowland, like the one she'd seen before,
So she beckoned all her generous friends across the office floor.

The letter read, 'Dear Santa, thank you so much for the cash,
My home is now so cosy and my water's warm to wash,
But I think I'd better tell you that your gift was ten pounds less
Than the hundred which I asked for, when I wrote to your address.

Now, I know you wouldn't cheat me, so I guess that, on the way,
The envelope was opened and a tenner slipped away;
To try to find the culprit? – Ach, would be to no avail,
But I'll bet it was some thieving cow in Belfast Royal Mail!'

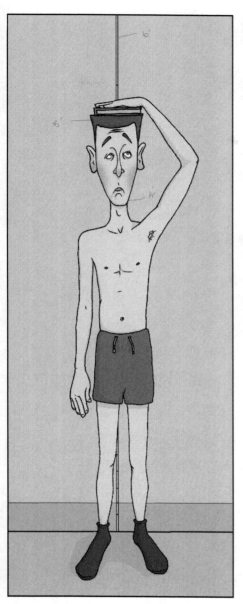

Military
Millimetres

a tall tale?

*M*any years ago, I met a man who claimed something like this had happened to him. I wasn't sure if I could believe him – and I don't think you'll believe the story about this fellow!

My name is Paddy Peters and I marksman skilled am I,
Me da taught me to fire a gun when I was three foot high;
Now, don't start thinkin' he did things like murder, robbin', lootin',
Naw, the thing me da was into is what's called clay pigeon shootin'.

So, let me introduce myself – I'm Paddy, as I've said,
And Pomeroy near Omagh is where I was born and bred;
I moved away to London, though, when I turned twenty-two,
Which brings me to the matter of the thing I'd love to do.

Hey, wait though, here's a wee bit on the last job that I had,
An attendant in a car park – ach, it wasn't all that bad;
I thought I looked so dapper in my dark blue uniform,
I'd brave that car park in the heat, the sleet, the snow, the storm!

I joined my local rifle club and showed them how to do it –
They had, in me, a champion, before they fully knew it!
But no success can compensate for what I want to be,
Sure, I'd make a crackin' *soldier* – but I'm only five-foot-three!

I've just loved all things military since I was knee-high
And, as for handling weapons, I've a marksman's eagle eye!
Why, I could be the dashing captain at a formal ball,
But then, to cut things short, there's just a thing 'bout being tall!

The problem is, for me, that had I grown just one inch more,

I'd be the shortest height they take – the magic five-foot-four!

But no matter, when they measured me in feet and centimetres,

The answer was the very same, 'You're too short, Mr Peters.'

Well, I was gutted! This just scuppered all I'd strived to do,

I couldn't stretch those centimetres up to one-six-two!

I'm sure they felt like laughing at me standing there forlorn,

As though they'd just encountered Ireland's largest leprechaun!

My granny came from Pittsburg and she said, 'You never know,

The *U.S. Army* might consider giving you a go!

So, visit their recruitment office, next year in the fall

When you go out to Idaho, to see your cousin, Paul!'

So, I went to the local base, to see what would ensue.

Why, I'd emigrate tomorrow, if I thought that it would do;

The sergeant looked me up and down, then gave a mighty sigh

Saying, 'First I'll need to check you're more than sixty inches high..

'Cos, buddy, even if you whizz through our tough ol' fitness test,

Your height might be an issue so, let's lay this thing to rest –

You tell me you're a marksman who has won a national cup?

Now I've gotta take your height, sir – let's see how you measure up!

You can be a baseball hero who's the talk of all Nebraska,
Or a national skating champion who's flown in from Alaska;
You can come from Alabama with a banjo on your knee,
But you can't join *this* army, pal, at only five-foot-three!'

Ach, dismayed, I journeyed homeward to the country of my birth
And asked, 'Is there a single army anywhere on earth
That might make all this effort that I'm going to worthwhile?'
Then, suddenly it dawned on me, 'Of course – *the Emerald Isle!*'

So, once back home, I headed off to Dublin with a smile
And said, 'The Irish Army's *perfect!* Sure, I'll pass in style!'
But no – the Captain shook his head, just like the ones before
Saying, 'Sorry, Mr Peters, you are not quite five-foot-four!'

I gasped, 'I thought you'd not recruit me if I was *too tall* –
I can't see how the *Irish Army* can be tall at all!
Why should it matter *here* that I am only *five-foot-three?*
Sure, our National Anthem starts by saying, *Soldiers are WEE!*'

Speaking of national anthems, when I was at school our teacher once asked the class, 'How do you know the Queen of England likes plums?' The answer, he said, was found in the words of the British National Anthem, where we have the line, 'Send her Victorias (victorious)!'

Like Your New View, Hugh? - *Phew!*

a tale with a whiff of caution...

This ballad finds its inspiration in a real-life dispute which developed between the owner of a pig farm and local residents. I thought there was enough material to 'sniff out' a tale!

My name's Hugh O'Farrell,
And here's my wife, Carol,
We bought that wee house up the lane;
We thought it looked nice
And at just the right price,
With a wonderful view of the Maine.

We'd lived in the city
But, like Walter Mitty,
Had dreamed of the improbable –
A rural retreat
In a setting so sweet,
Like a painting by John Constable!

Then, when we retired,
We both felt inspired
To follow our dream and uproot
To a cottage so quaint
Where Carol could paint
And I would grow veggies and fruit.

So, here we are now,

Just under the bough

Of a sycamore tree in full leaf

And our very own field

With soil that will yield

Ten sackfuls of spuds from beneath!

It was five years ago

When we thought we would go

For a drive in the country one day;

It was just after lunch

And we both had a hunch

That, after we left the cafe,

'Fore our walk on the sand,

We should just head inland

To see if some properties might

Be for sale, for the trick

Was to get in real quick,

So we didn't miss one that was right!

Well, suddenly Carol
Screamed, 'Hughie O'Farrell!
Just look at what house has a sign –
With its fresh sky-blue paint,
And a setting so quaint,
It's a cottage I'd love to call mine!'

As I'd noticed it too,
Without further ado
We stopped and went up to the door;
Though no viewing was booked,
They were fine that we looked:
'You're welcome to see around more.'

Well, on viewing we found
The cottage was sound,
With not one repair job to do;
We loved every inch,
But the main thing to clinch
It, was seeing that wonderful view!

Through a large window pane
Our eyes followed the lane
Past the farmer constructing a shed,
'Cross the river and meadow
And cornfields of yellow
To faraway hills, dark as lead.

Well, it was such a vision,
We made the decision
To sell up at once and move here
And, when three months went by
We were in, home and dry,
Enjoying the new atmosphere!

We talked and we dreamed,
Our new freedom, it seemed
Was like we'd been granted a pardon –
Carol thought she'd sell crafts
And I looked up some drafts
For building a small market garden!

With the fresh country air
And an outlook so rare
And the pace of our lives rearranged,
Plus the garden's sweet scent,
We were both so content.
That was, until *everything* changed!

For, one morning in May
It seemed such a nice day
When we woke, Carol said, 'Listen, Hugh,
To the song of the thrush,
Just like us, in no rush,'
And then, without further ado,

With a song in her head
She got out of the bed
And opened the window to see
Our marvellous view,
Then she gasped, 'Oh, no – Hugh!'
And slammed it with some urgency!

So, I rushed to her side
And, with eyes opened wide
We saw, with increasing alarm
That our neighbour, young Fred
Who'd built that huge shed,
Had done it to start a *pig farm!*

Now, as most people know,
Once *that's* on the go
The smell is like nothing on earth!
Sheep and cattle are fine,
But talk about *swine* –
Well, tuppence was all we were worth!

From that day, we felt trapped
And poor Carol, she flapped
All about her – the smell drove her daft;
Our dream, I declare
Had become a nightmare,
As around us such odour would waft!

So, the windows stayed shut!
Ach now, I'll tell you what –
We couldn't risk opening them wide
For, once opened a bit,
Even just a wee slit,
The stench of that farm got inside!

Now, outside? Don't mention!
The smell caused great tension
'Tween Carol and me – please don't ask!
She just sat and cried
While I got up and tried
To search for my dad's old gas mask!

Well, as summer drew near
And the heat rose, oh, dear –
The stench just got stronger each day;
Blood pressure was raised –
We sat down and appraised
Our dilemma and where relief lay.

'Hugh, this won't improve,
I think we should move,'
Said Carol, now at tether's end;
I replied, 'Try to *sell it?*
Once visitors *smell it,*
No cash they'll be wanting to spend!

Sure, they'll be in some hurry
To get from that slurry
And breathe clear, fresh air once again;
It seems like we're stuck
With the smell of this muck –
It's sure one ridiculous pain!'

But, when there seemed no hope,
We started to cope –
Carol sells *scented candles* galore,
And my market garden?
Its smell you must pardon –
Wild Garlic's the *sole* herb in store!

Joe Ormo

a tale from a youngster's viewpoint...

This isn't so much a barmy ballad as a poem based on a true – and autobiographical – story from my boyhood. Joe was indeed a real person whom I thought looked a lot like President Kennedy. (Bread vans were commonplace in the 1960s, the Ormo Bakery in Belfast being one of the biggest producers and distributors).

When some great story breaks that has importance monumental,
A happening to shock us all, so deeply consequential,
It's said that, for some unknown reason, we will never lose
The memory of where we were when we first heard the news.

A case that's often quoted is the death of JFK,
When the President was shot in Dallas on that fateful day;
And, though I hope you might be thinking I seem far too youthful,
Yes, I remember where I was, to be completely truthful!

It was the house where I grew up and we'd just finished tea
On the twenty-second of November 1963;
As TV news went round the world of his assassination,
I watched it sitting on the floor, with childlike fascination.

The significance of that event, of course, was lost on me,
For I was just a little lad way back in '63;
But Kennedy's was certainly a face I'd come to know
And said, 'Hey, someone's shot that man who looks a lot like Joe!'

Joe was the Ormo bread man, whose van came round each week,
A friendly, chatty bloke who always took the time to speak
To customers both young and old, and he reminded me
Of that man in the news each evening, John F. Kennedy.

Joe was bright and breezy, with a word for everyone,
And I imagined that he'd have an eager sense of fun;
Popular and punctual, neither grumpy nor erratic,
I'd say that, like his doppelganger, Joe was charismati c!

That just about sums up what I recall of JFK
And the memory I still possess of that most dreadful day;
It's funny, though, to think the reason it's still in my head
Is because he looked so like the man who brought the Ormo bread!

Does *Joe* remember where *he* was when he first heard the news,
If he's still with us, and that memory's one you never lose?
Perhaps *he* called out to his wife, just as they finished tea,
'Hey, someone's gone and shot that man who looks a lot like me!'

Buses, Baccy and
Bolts of Lightning!

an electrifying tale...

And now for a truly surreal story! This 'current' tale explains itself as it goes along – and just gets increasingly crazier!

At Arthur's Court in Camelot, steeped in the mists of time,
The great Magician Merlin did recite a magic rhyme
Intended to transport him to a future day, from whence
He could foresee if Arthur's foes had all been driven hence.

Now Merlin, though advanced in years, possessed a skill so great
That often his own powerfulness he'd underestimate
And, so it was that forward through the ages he was flung –
And landed on the Crumlin Road in nineteen-sixty-one!

At once, he knew that refuge he must seek until the spell
Wore off, then back to Camelot he'd hurtle, safe and well;
A sign placed close beside him read, 'King's Hall: Route Seventeen'
So Merlin said, 'That's where I'll find this city's lord or queen.'

With flowing cloak and pointed hat, he soon became aware
That, as he strode along, all passers-by would stop and stare;
Just then he overheard two folk say, if you want no fuss,
The quickest means of travel is a thing that they call 'bus'.

He walked towards a little shelter, where he saw a sign
That read, 'Bus Stop', and there stood several people in a line;
By now he'd formed an image, in a basic sense, of course,
Of a huge, red iron vehicle that did not require a horse.

Now, in a bus not far away, a man called Sammy Brown
Was taking fares from passengers all bound for Belfast town;
Of all the bus conductors, he was known both far and wide
For a grumpy disposition, that just couldn't be denied.

Conductors on the buses were, in general, cheerful guys,
With friendly chat for everyone and laughter in their eyes,
But as for old Brown? Not a chance! He'd simply make you groan;
Impatient, cross and often rude, all Sammy did was moan.

Well, if his manner didn't irk his passengers enough,
He always chewed tobacco and smelt strongly of the stuff
And, of course, of all the buses in the whole of Belfast town,
The one old Merlin climbed on board was that of Sammy Brown!

'Take me to your monarch's castle,' Merlin boldly said,
To which old Brown replied, 'Hey, oul lad, are ye off yer head?
Speak up, man – where's yer money and just where ye goin' to?
This bus goes down to York Street, then up Royal Avenue!'

'Did you say *Royal* Avenue? I prithee, plainly tell,'
Said Merlin, 'if that is the place wherein thy rulers dwell.'
'I don't know what yer on about,' snarled Brown, 'but listen, pop,
If you don't talk some common sense, you're off at our next stop!'

'Do *you* know whom you do address?' asked Merlin. 'Understand,
If you make threats towards me, I'll be forced to use my wand!'
'I don't know where you're going, with that garb and long white hair,'
Snapped Brown, 'but you've ten seconds, mate, to magic up a fare!'

At that, the wizard took his wand and aimed it, straight and good,
Yet Sammy showed no fear and calmly some tobacco chewed;
Then Merlin fired a lightning bolt, with one almighty shout,
But short of frying Sammy Brown, it merely fizzled out!

On seeing that his foe still breathed, the old magician gasped
And roared another incantation, whilst his wand he clasped.
Two posh old dears said, 'Funny accent; must be from the south,'
Whilst Sammy, unperturbed, popped more tobacco in his mouth!

Just as before, the second bolt of lightning did no harm,
It simply came to nothing and caused Sammy no alarm;
Now, just to see what happened next, most folk would walk a mile
As, for the first time ever known, old Sammy broke a smile!

Well, Merlin was indeed perplexed, yet one more time he tried
To zap old Sammy – now this battle was a test of pride!
Wee Aggie turned to her friend Vi and whispered, 'Poor oul crater;
Must be somethin' wrong wi' him - should take him to the Mater!'

'I simply do not comprehend; the bolt will always strike,'
Sighed Merlin. 'Of such strong resistance, I've not seen the like!'
'Right, Wizard,' Sammy said, 'I hope you like it here, because
I don't know when the next bus comes to take you back to Oz!'

So, off he ushered Merlin, just beside the Co-Op store,
And, 'Puff!' the Wizard's spell was gone and he was seen no more;
'I'm glad you're back,' King Arthur said. 'Now drive my foes away!'
'I'll turn them into toads,' he said. 'Bolt lightning's off today!'

Now back in Belfast, everyone was mystified full well,
And started to discuss how Sammy broke old Merlin's spell;
Some thought he'd just been lucky, but most said they didn't know,
While others asked if chewing baccy stopped the current's flow.

Yet Sammy, strangely, through it all, had seemed quite self-assured,
Despite the great electric currents he had just endured,
As if he knew that lightning bolts of such velocity
Would fail to generate sufficient electricity!

Then the driver of the double-decker, Alastair McNabb
Turned round and shouted to him from inside his driver's cab:
'The tobacco didn't save you, Sam, nor was it your good luck. Sir,
As everyone in Belfast knows – you're just a bad *conductor!*'

Who's in the Driving Seat?

a sheepdog's 'tail'...

I heard another 'old yarn' and thought it would make a good poem! I think this one's quite believable, as there's a quick, dry wit in the humour of folk here which manifests itself in all sorts of circumstances.

The M.O.T. (Ministry Of Transport) test must be given to older vehicles annually, to ensure they're roadworthy.

Oul Wullie John McAllister was drivin' home one night
In yon oul skip he calls a car, that's yellow, blue and white;
His bold wee collie, Bob, was lyin' sleepin' in the back,
When two young peelers pulled him in to do a routine check.

'Good evening, sir,' the first one said. 'Now, sir, is this your car?'
'I'd like tay think so,' Wullie smiled, 'been in it this last hour.
If I'd been out to steal a car, in your opinion, miss,
D'ye no' think I'd have taken a far better yin than *this*?'

Of course the polis pulled him in, they felt they had no option
For Wullie John's car was, to all, a funny oul contraption –
He'd change the bits that wore out, be they bonnet, wheel or door,
With new parts that were nothing like the ones he'd had before!

They looked it up and down and read the discs and documents,
But shook their heads, as what they saw made not a bit of sense,
For once they'd checked it out, the police could very quickly see
To their amazement, Wullie's car had passed its M.O.T!

'Now, may I see your *licence*, sir?' the young policewoman asked
And, once again, in every detail, Wullie John soon passed;
Not one endorsement had he got, in fifty years of drivin',
'Now let me on,' oul Wullie snapped. 'Enough o' this connivin'!'

'Your licence, sir, is fine,' she said, 'so we'll not keep you back,
But I see that this dog of yours has no tag round his neck;
Now, does he have a licence, sir? He *must* have one, you see.'
'No need,' he said. 'Bob just leaves all the drivin' up tay me!'

Footnote: *In Ireland, you must have a licence to keep a dog.*

Mathematical Metamorphosis

a numerical tale...

This poem's set in a slower tempo and revolves around the contrasting interests of a middle-aged suburban couple. It's an example of how even the most ordinary of situations can be developed into a piece of poetry.

On a quiet road in Howth lived Liz and Peter, the O'Learys,
Who met each other years back, 'neath the famous clock at Clerys;
They both worked hard and sent their kids to university,
But then Liz felt her lifestyle needed more diversity.
Like many folk, she'd had her share of worry, sweat and tears
And now was settling down, with Pete, into those middle years.
A sensible, well-balanced couple, Liz a dietitian
And Peter a most passionate and expert… mathematician!

Now, everything was good, there was no problem, big or small
With the state of Liz and Peter's marriage – nothing wrong at all;
So, don't misunderstand me – Liz was no frustrated wife,
But she hankered after something that might just spice up her life!
'I feel that, now the kids have gone, well, things are kind of static,
And Pete? He just loves anything remotely mathematic,'
She said. 'Just something in my life – a welcome intermission
Would do; I don't get off on being an expert mathematician!'

Well, through their letterbox one day in flopped the morning post;
The usual ads and bills, of course, accounted for the most
Of what Liz had to deal with, then one letter caught her eye –
She must have read it seven times, not stopping to ask why.
It said, 'You're one of thirty thousand entered for a prize –
A holiday so wonderful, you won't believe your eyes!'
Said Liz, 'The thought of winning that is just pure supposition,
But stuff the odds! I've never been an expert mathematician!'

So, hoping that her luck was in, Liz sent the coupon off,
Though once she mentioned it to Pete, he struggled not to scoff
And, being very logical, he thought perhaps he'd better
Explain why not to rest such hope upon this kind of letter:
'Enter if you want to, but you'll have to be content
To know the chance is only nought-point-nought-nought-five percent;
Please sit down for a moment, dear and now, with your permission,
I'll show you what this looks like to an expert mathematician!'

Well, two or three weeks after this, another letter came,

Sent by a different company, but similar, just the same.

It said, 'You're one of forty thousand entered for a draw

To win a car worth fifty grand!' This filled her full of awe!

Again, Pete said, 'Feel free, but just remember, the event

Of Liz O'Leary winning is well under one percent;

Sit down here for a moment – with a little repetition,

I'll show you how to do this like an expert mathematician!'

Now, as the months went by, Liz found a new prize draw each week,

And, as for *Pete*, he labelled her a competition geek!

Sometimes she'd try to justify each single minute spent

For, once or twice, she made it to the final ten percent!

But Pete, forever practical, was there with page and pencil

To say, 'My dear, some grounding in Pure Maths is quite essential;

They'll tell you that you've got a chance in every competition,

But this is what the odds are, to an expert mathematician!

Then, eventually, one day in March, *another* letter came,
It offered some amazing prize – ach, virtually the same
As all the ones preceding it: 'This draw will change your life!'
So again, Pete fetched a pencil to explain things to his wife;
But, before he pulled his chair up, *Liz had done it in her head,*
And, impressed by her quick calculation, Pete so calmly said,
'These letters, dear, *have* changed your life beyond all recognition –
'Tween them and me, *you've* now become an expert mathematician!'

Patrick's Prayer

a boy's tale...

There's a bit of humour mixed with pathos in this prayer of a nine-year-old boy. I've tried to keep things close to what a youngster of this age might say, as children sometimes display an honesty that's lacking in grown-ups!

Dear God, it's Patrick here, aged nine,
Please listen to this prayer of mine;
Although I'm young and very small,
I hope you'll want to hear it all.

I'm sure so *many* people pray,
You must hear *millions* every day
From...France to...Ireland to...Hong Kong,
So I'll try not to keep you long!

Lord, thank you for the food we eat,
Like sausages and luncheon meat,
But I would lie if I told you
That I like sprouts and cabbage too!

In church last Sunday, Bishop Quinn
Said we must confess our sin;
I *don't* think I am way *too* bad,
But *mum* says I can drive her mad!

I made a list of sins I've done,
Though some were just a bit of fun;
I'll get my list out of your way –
My *sister's* list might take all day!

Please bless my teacher, Mrs Bass
And all the children in my class,
But I will *never* like John Toole –
Please move him to another school!

Bless James and, uh... *okay* – Marie,
Our mum calls us her terrible three;
Please help *him* not to be so lazy,
And help *her* not to drive *us* crazy!

The Bishop told us, from our birth
And, all around this whole big earth
That *every* child is loved by you –
Does that include my *sister*, too?

It's Christmas soon – I'm being good,
Help me behave the way I should;
I really want that Star Wars Jenga
So you'll know I can't risk mum's anger!

Lord, please help James to be good, too
And do the things he's meant to do,
Then he will get a Curve Crossbow
And he might let *me* have a go!

About my sister – I'm not sure
If her behaviour we can cure;
Just watch her closely and you'll see
If she deserves an MP3!

And, oh yes – please bless Mum and Gran
And Auntie Clare and Uncle Dan;
I know they boss and moan and fuss,
Yet I'm glad they look after us.

But sometimes, God, it makes me sad
That Mum no longer lives with Dad;
I love them both and wish that they
Could still be friends, so dad would stay.

I heard mum say to Auntie Clare
That she found out Dad had a fair;
She says he has a roving eye,
Er... is that something like a stye?

I think we should send Dad a letter
To wish his eye will soon get better
And hope that, if he has a fair,
He'll sell nice cakes and chutney there.

When I fight with my brother James
And sometimes call him nasty names,
Soon after we have had that fight
I give him sweets and it's alright.

So I pray that you'll help Mum see
How things work out with James and me
And, if she gives Dad sweets to chew
The pair of them might make up, too.

Then, on the TV news each night
We see how quickly people fight;
I ask that, just like James and me,
World leaders might learn to agree.

Well, God, without your help, I guess
We'd all be in a bigger mess,
So I think what we all should do
Is ask that we grow more like you!

Frank

a commercial tale...

Frank was a real-life wheeler-and-dealer known to one of my fellow writers. I wrote this piece using what facts I'd learned about him and added a few details of my own. The scene opens as Frank introduces himself to a couple living in a rather expensive area. There's a fair bit of bletherin', as I heard Frank really had 'the gift of the gab'!

I'm Francis O'Fee, but 'Frank' they call me;
Now, how are you doin', yourselves?
Ach, you're lookin' right well an' I think I can tell
There's a bargain or two on your shelves!
I'm sure your home's nifty, I reckon you're thrifty,
You'd never do anythin' rash,
And I bet yer heart's sinkin'; yer sayin', 'He's thinkin'
O' fiddlin' us out o' some cash!'
Now, just hear me spiel – I give a good deal
And there's no *skullduggery* planned;
I just get a great feelin' from wheelin' an' dealin'
An' the chance o' some cash in me hand!

Ach, I acted the fool! I used to bunk school
An' learned all I knew on the street;
Drove me ma round the bend, so she always would send
Me, by bike, to buy something to eat.
Well now, I used to park it down by the market
And started to think it was fun
To hear the guys barter, an' grew all the smarter
By watchin' how tradin' was done!
Then I served on the floor of a furniture store,
But workin' there, I couldn't stand,
But I got a great feelin' from wheelin' an' dealin'
An' the chance o' some cash in me hand!

I was late home one day after I got me pay –
I'd spent the lot in a shebeen;
With a curse and a clout, me ma turfed me out
An' me just a lad of eighteen!
If I'd stayed in the Pale, I'd have ended in jail
So I made up me mind there an' then
That, without any fuss, I'd hop on the bus
To Belfast; I'd heard able men
Could find a good job. Well, I made a fair bob
An' the odd nice wee nixer was grand,
For I got a great feelin' from wheelin' an' dealin'
An' the chance o' some cash in me hand!

Still, for all o' me life I've had the same wife,
A wee girl I met in Dungloe;
It's a marvel how she ever put up wi' me
An' six kids in our wee terrace row!
She worked as a dancer but married this chancer
An' stuck wi' him through thick an' thin,
Yet I've always been able to put bread on table
By *some* means – now is that a sin?
Some don't like me, I'm sure, but I'm not a cute hoor,
I'm respected all over the land,
An' I get a great feelin' from wheelin' an' dealin'
An' the chance o' some cash in me hand!

Now, though Brenda will mutter, I like a wee flutter!

Sure, it's not on the list o' top crimes

To place a few bob that I've earned from me job

On a horse, an' the oul Racin' Times

Is my handbook for life (don't be tellin' the wife),

An' the rare week that money is flowin'

I'll skedaddle – no traces, to those Galway Races

Without that wee wife o' mine knowin'!

Backed a winner called Hubbard, went out an' got fluthered,

Then came home an' bought a new van,

For I get a great feelin' from wheelin' an' dealin'

An' the chance o' some cash in me hand!

Now, I'll tell you no joke, but a lot o' posh folk,

When seein' me van round their blocks,

Think that I'm some oul goat in a long, grey, tweed coat

An' a hat over fadin' brown locks.

Sure, I look worse for wear but I'm gifted, I swear

At spottin' a bargain or two,

And I'll never impose, but right under your nose

There might be a bob, if you knew!

Can I call you a friend? Then, I won't offend

You with cheap offers made to demand,

Though I still get that feelin' from wheelin' an' dealin'

And the chance o' some cash in me hand!

Now, there's *no* way I'd pressure you, but some oul dresser
Or maybe an oul rockin' chair
Might fetch a fine price if it's still lookin' nice
An' the deal that I'll do will be fair!
Ach, I'm not some rich man in his big maroon van,
But an honest lad, if there was one;
Sure, I've no bank account an' don't know the amount
O' savin' that I've ever done.
Well, you might think I'm funny wi' me wad o' money
Rolled up in a strong rubber band,
It's just part o' the feelin' o' wheelin' an' dealin'
And the chance o' some cash in me hand!

But, it sure breaks me heart if me customers start
To doubt every word that I say;
Some don't know Frank O'Fee an' they try to con *me* –
Sure, I deal wi' their sort every day!
There's the *odd* porky pie - just a *little* white lie,
If they spin me a yarn that's not true;
But, I like to be straight, I'll pay fair goin' rate
When dealin' wi' nice folk like you!
Sure, it's grand to build trust, but I must earn me crust,
Ach, I hope that you might understand;
I just get a great feelin' from wheelin' an' dealin'
An' the chance o' some cash in me hand!

Well, I'll take me leave soon. Now, you're – *Brian and June?*
An' what's your wee dog called – a *Chow?*
But, before it's goodbye, is there anythin' I
Might have a wee gander at now?
I'll spin you no guff an' I'll pay well enough
For somethin' you'd like to discard;
Now you're suckin' diesel if I buy an' *re*-sell
Some oul crock left out in your yard!
On a deal we might shake – you'll be glad you could make
A bob that's been wholly unplanned,
Sure, *you'll* get a great feelin' from wheelin' an' dealin'
An' the chance o' some cash in your hand!

A Spinster, a Sister, a Signal, a Skid, a Shopping Mall, Smash–Up...and Sergeant!

a tale for all motorists...

Miss Constance Cleary (88) was out for a drive and suddenly jammed on her brakes as the traffic lights ahead turned green! Skidding into a shopping centre and causing mayhem to shoppers and staff, Miss Cleary was unhurt and somewhat oblivious to what she'd done. As we join the story, Sgt. Brian O'Leary from the local police station has just arrived to investigate the incident and what follows is the conversation between them.

'You've driven your car through a shopping mall's door,
Knocked lots of merchandise over the floor
And injured three people – it could have been more;
Please tell me what happened, Miss Cleary.'

'I first lost control at the junction outside,
Jammed on my brakes and just started to slide
Towards this big store, where I landed inside.
That's all I know, Sergeant O'Leary.'

'So, you tried to stop suddenly, ma'am, is that right?
Was there something that happened to give you a fright?
Did a dawdling pedestrian come into sight?
Please give me more detail, Miss Cleary.'

'My sister of ninety's out driving today,
And I always try hard to stay out of Dot's way
As, towards traffic signals, she's rather blasé;
That's the real reason, Sergeant O'Leary.'

'The point you've just made, ma'am, you'll have to explain,
I'm afraid that, to me, it sounds somewhat arcane.
About Dot your sister – please tell me again
Where *she* fits into all this, Miss Cleary.'

'Well, you know when you see traffic lights up ahead?
Dot never will stop when the lights are turned red,
Yet if they turn green, she just stops the car dead
Every time. Bless her, Sergeant O'Leary!'

'So, she moves when they're red and she stops when they're green?
Now, ma'am, you've done likewise, from what I have seen,
And a reason I'll need, if you see what I mean,
So think slowly and tell me, Miss Cleary.'

'Well, when it was red, I knew I was okay
But, once it turned green, I was wiser to stay,
In case Dot was coming the opposite way –
I put SAFETY first, Sergeant O'Leary!'

Padlocks In Poland

a tale from Krakow...

*'**W**hat's a poem about **Poland** doing in a book of **Irish** ballads?' you might ask! (It's something which could only happen in Ireland, isn't it?) Well, many Polish (and other European) people live in Ireland today and make a valuable contribution to Irish society. I hope that if you're from Poland (or indeed Ireland!) you like this light-hearted story taking place against the backdrop of a famous Krakow festival. (Iza is pronounced 'Eeza').*

'Twas the night of Kupala in downtown Krakow,
When Marek and Iza (whose name means 'God's Vow'),
Met in a car-park and had a big row!

She was off to the Light-and-Sound Concert that hour
And, while crossing a car-park, near Wanda's Wine Bar
Walked straight in the path of an on-coming car.

'Hey, look where you're going!' an angry voice said.
'Keep walking like that, girl and soon you'll be dead!'
Then Iza composed herself, lifting her head.

She said, 'Hoi, there, Marek, stop driving so fast,
I don't want this evening to end up my last,
Or hobble for six months in some plaster-cast!'

'Well, aren't you a cross one,' said Marek, so smug,
'Now, give me a smile and a nice little hug
And I'll drive you away in my trendy *Love Bug*!'

'It may be a *Love Bug* to *some* girls you see,'
Said Iza, 'but fast cars just don't impress *me*;
Now, if you don't mind, there's a place I've to be.'

But Marek replied, 'Can I help that I'm cool,
So handsome and charming and nobody's fool,
And the best *ever* student when I was at school?

And I've got the trendiest car in Krakow,
No wonder the girls stare at me and go, "Wow!"
At least *ten* young ladies would jump in here now!'

'Whatever,' said Iza, 'I'll bid you goodbye,
I really don't know if I should laugh or cry;
You're rather pathetic. I just want to sigh!

This Eve of Saint John, every girl casts her wreath
As part of *wianki*, to Wisla beneath,
And hopes that, with cunning and speed like a thief..

..A young man of honour will snatch her wreath out
From the flow of the river that bobs it about,
Which makes *him* her true love, without any doubt!

You're just out to *flirt* with the girls near and far
By picking them up at the trendiest bar
And spinning them round in your sleek motor car.

So, Marek,' said Iza, 'I'll let you enjoy
Speeding round in your car – I will get a nice boy
Who can win my heart over without some dear toy!'

'I'm sorry that you think so lowly of me,'
Said Marek, 'but jump in and you'll quickly see
That a boy with my charm doesn't need *wianki.*'

Then Marek laughed loudly and Marek laughed long,
'Oh, Iza, you're funny, though totally wrong
To think that some fellow so dashing and strong..

..Will down to the riverbank stealthily creep
To pull out your wreath from the waters so deep!
Go back to your dreams, girl – it's just in your sleep!'

'You've no sense of romance!' she snapped, with a frown,
'And here you are living in this Polish town
That's well recognised for romantic renown!

And you are so arrogant!' young Iza said.
'Just having this car has gone right to your head;
Hey, why don't you try being nicer instead?'

'I'm nice as I am,' Marek quipped, with a grin,
'But I see that your heart is a hard one to win,
So, I'll bid you goodnight, now – I'm off for a spin!'

'Oh, what a big ego!' said Iza, out loud,
'I don't think I've ever met someone so proud.'
And then she walked on, to her friends in the crowd.

Now, Iza disliked Marek's arrogant mood
And, whilst running the risk of appearing quite rude,
Avoided the fellow as much as she could.

But, Marek? A challange he'd never resist
And, determined his presence would not be dismissed,
He'd soon have *that* girl driven, dated and kissed!

And so, Marek bet with his friends in the bar
That, by next Kupala, though it seemed quite far,
He'd surely entice Iza into his car!

Well, when the next Eve of Saint John drew quite near,
To her friends, Iza said, 'If I find true love dear,
We will walk to the bridge over Wisla, so clear!'

Now, the place Iza spoke of was that very same
Father Bernatek Footbridge, where all couples came
To fasten a padlock inscribed with their name..

..And then toss the key to the water below
And in doing, their true love to all the world show;
Well, that is where Iza declared she would go.

So, once the great night came, with all of her friends,
Iza walked to the river, the part where it bends
But with no thought of Marek, or making amends.

Well, the girls cast their wreaths on the water, so wide
And watched if they'd travel, or drift to the side,
Then suddenly, with great excitement, they cried..

..As, stealthily, out came a man who was masked,
And, while all assembled there audibly gasped,
From close to the bank, Iza's bright wreath he grasped!

Well Iza, quite stunned, said, 'Though I can't tell who
This man is, I know that the thing I must do
Is follow my heart. To my word I'll be true!'

So, with great excitement, yet mingled with fear,
As her secret suitor's steps brought him up near,
She tried to stay calmer than she might appear.

Then, he pulled off his mask without making a sound,
And, as a great scream from the crowd did resound,
Poor Iza's jaw almost dropped down to the ground!

She couldn't believe it was *Marek* who'd dared
To play the great hero and, more cross than scared,
For the sake of her word, she'd do what she'd declared.

Without further ado, to the footbridge they walked,
Though scarcely a sentence to Marek she talked;
Indeed, Iza felt that she'd truly been stalked..

..And, to make matters worse, all that Marek would do
Was boast of his money and flashy car, too,
And tell her, 'My front seat is ready for you!'

Well, once they arrived on the bridge, Iza said,
'Right, here is the padlock, I'll do what I said,'
And scratched on their names with a nail, old and red.

She opened the lock with a large metal key,
But Marek then snatched it and said, 'Allow me!'
And fastened it onto the bridge with much glee.

Well, Iza just shook her head – worse would ensue;
Said Marek, 'My car's in the square – don't feel blue,
For many a girl would just love to be you!'

'Let's do this bit properly,' Iza replied,
That key you just stuffed down your pocket, inside
Is meant to be thrown in the river, so wide!

'You're right,' answered Marek, 'How could I forget?'
And searched in his pocket until he found it,
Then quickly he threw it to depths cold and wet.

Now, unknown to Iza, bold Marek had made
An additional bet on this whole escapade
That by ten o'clock sharp he would have his fair maid..

..In the seat of his car, so this bet would be won,
For the challenge to him just amounted to fun,
And no woman in Krakow *his* presence would shun!

Well, Iza knew something was up, in the square –
She saw Marek's friends all applauding him there
But telling him he'd only seconds to spare!

He quickly whisked Iza to his latest car
And told her that, rather than feeling bizarre,
Inside it, she'd think she's a real movie star!

But just as the town clock struck: *one two, three, four…*
Marek grew flustered, and then panicked more,
As he found his key wouldn't open the door!

Well, the hour now was over, the deadline was crossed,
And Marek was beaten, his bet had been lost;
Laughed Iza, 'You realise now what you tossed?

You're not so smart, Marek, as we can all see,
You bungled things up on the bridge there with me,
Digging deep in your pocket to find that old key.

For, *winning your bet* was so much in your head,
It's the key of the *padlock* you're holding instead,
And *your* key? – It's down on the deep river bed!'

The Rocky Road to Dublin?
- It's a rockier journey home!

a tale two folk wish hadn't
taken place...

*B*ack to Ireland again for this last ballad which, believe it or not,
is based on an actual story!

Two mates called Jack and Tommy, back in nineteen-sixty-three
Drove from Belfast town to Dublin – a football match to see;
They got two grandstand tickets in the former Lansdowne Road
And, like all avid fans that day they rattled, cheered and crowed!

Now, once the match was over, Jack and Tommy sauntered in
For a quick pint in a Dublin pub, to celebrate the win;
They verbally replayed the game, then Tommy said, 'Hey, Jack,
Just take a look behind you – see who's sittin' at the back!'

There, in a quiet corner, slumped and sleeping in a chair
Was a certain man from Belfast looking much the worse for wear.
'It's wee Dan Kearney – Mary's man, from Ponderosa Street,'
Said Jack. 'Looks like he'll have a job to get back on his feet!'

'Aw, poor oul crater,' Tommy said, 'he's had too much to drink;
If *we'd* known he was at the match, ach, Jack, I'd like to think
We would've brought him down wi' us and, listen, I'm just thinkin'
We might have kept him sober, knowin' what he's like for drinkin'!'

'Wake up, mate!' he shouted. 'Dan! It's Tommy here, with Jack;
You've had a wee bit much to drink, but we can drive you back!
We'll get you into Jack's car, mate, where you can rest your head.'
'But,' whispered Jack, 'when Mary sees him, he's as good as dead!'

So, sprawled across the back seat of Jack's trusty Standard Ten,
Dan slept the whole way back to Belfast, where his two mates then
With some degree of difficulty got him on his feet,
And dragged him up to his front door in Ponderosa Street.

They rang the bell and held their breath; both knew what lay in store
For wee Dan, once his Mary got him in through that front door
But, instead of *Mary* standing there, it was his daughter, Joan.
Jack said, 'Love, here's yer da – he'd not have made it on his own.'

'He's had a bit too much to drink,' said Tommy. 'Just the same,
It's good we saw him – there were thousands at that football game!
Well, that's him home. Just mind the step; I think you'll need to watch
Him on the stairs, love – let's just hope that he enjoyed the match!'

'*What* match?' she asked them, mystified. 'Whatever do you mean?
He went to Dublin, sure, but Lansdowne Rd's not where he's been;
Don't think that I'm not grateful to you, bringing home me da,
But I've a question for you – can you tell me, where's me *ma*?

Me ma and da went down to Dublin on the mornin' train
To do their Christmas shoppin' and, I swear, she made it plain
To him there'd be no drinkin' – he was there to help her shop,
And that she'd have his life if he as much as touched one drop!'

Now, meanwhile, down in Dublin, can you guess who's going mad?
Well, of course poor Mary can't find hide nor hair of wee Joan's dad;
She searched the length of Grafton St, then up round Parnell Square
But it seemed as if her Dan had disappeared into thin air!

Sure, she'd left him sitting on a bench and told him to stay put
While she went into Clerys Store to buy a winter suit;
Now, Mary took a little while to find her shade of green
And, when she came back out, wee Dan was nowhere to be seen!

'I knew it – He's gone drinkin!' Mary hissed, in muffled rage,
And called him by a few choice names that can't go on this page;
Well, in and out of every bar she barged and stormed until
Of tiredness and exasperation, she'd just had her fill!

Now, remember, this was long before we had the mobile phone,
So she hurried to a call box, where she pressed the dialling tone;
Well, slowly she got through to Joan, who told her all the craic –
How Jack and Tommy found her da and brought him, legless, back.

Now, you won't need *me* to tell you just how flamin' mad she was:
'I swear, I'll throttle him tonight,' screamed Mary, 'all because
I leave him for ten minutes, thinking he can't wander far
And he ends up in *Belfast,* 'cos he's walked into a bar!'

Then, carrying her heavy bag, with arms and legs in pain,
She realised she'd *minutes* left to catch the Belfast train
And, gasping for each breath and lacking all co-ordination,
Mary reached the platform gate at Connolly Railway Station.

Well, exhausted from her awful trip and feeling she could die,
Mary flopped down in the train and heaved a mighty sigh
Then, setting down her shopping bag and kicking off her shoes,
She thought, 'At least I'm going home. I swear I'll need to snooze!'

Now, it wasn't long before the train conductor came around
And startled Mary: 'Ma'am, is that your ticket on the ground?'
'Uhuh!' she said, still half asleep. 'That's mine, the date is right –
I had to run to catch this train so I'd get home tonight!'

'Your ticket is for Belfast, ma'am,' he said, with some concern.
'That's right,' said Mary, 'I went in and got a day's return.'
'I see it's valid,' he replied, 'but I would risk a guess
You don't know that the train you're on's the *Limerick Express!*'

Well, Mary just burst into tears – could things get any worse?
Her shopping day round Dublin stores had now become a curse;
The train that she was travelling on turned out to be the last,
And hurtling all the way to Limerick – nowhere near Belfast!

She rummaged madly through her bag to find a pound or two;
With just enough for one more fare, the only thing to do
Was find a place to sit all night, then catch the morning train
To Dublin, where she'd make the switch to get back home again.

Of course the hour was late when Mary got to Limerick town
And it was hard to find a place where she could settle down;
To top it all, the heavens opened – boy, the rain did pelt her,
'Till finally she stumbled – drenched – into a wee bus shelter.

Well, morning came and, with her trip so horribly bedevilled,
Not having slept, she got her train, though looking wild dishevelled;
Yet, with a chill now starting, and exhausted through-and-through,
She swore, 'I'll kill that Dan if it's the last thing that I do!'

And so, hours later, back in Belfast she arrived, dead beat
And walked, bedraggled, to her home in Ponderosa Street;
But, still, before Joan drew her breath to ask, 'How are ye, ma?'
With all her might, our Mary bellowed, 'Right, girl, where's yer da?'

'Well, ma,' Joan answered, 'it's like this, he's been away all day;
He left the house this morning with the most of next week's pay
Then, with a right wee stagger and a head that felt like two,
He caught the first train back to Dublin, ma, to search for *you!*'

Glossary:

'Ach, dry ye'er eyes!' / "An' go an' boil ye'er heed': 'Stop complaining!' / 'Get lost!' ('Heed' = head / 'reed' = 'red).

Bargin': Barging is a word for scolding often used around Belfast.

Blarney: nonsensical, humorous talk, sometimes used to charm or trick the listeners. Kissing the 'Blarney Stone' on the battlements of Blarney Castle in County Cork is said to endow everyone one with 'the gift of the gab' (eloquence in speech).

Blether: to talk a lot of nonsense, particularly in a long-winded way.

Brave wee man: a decent fellow.

Bunk school: play truant.

Clock at Clerys: Clerys was a department store in Dublin with a clock on its wall which was famous as a rendezvous point and traditionally a spot where romances begin.

Co-Op: for many years, the Co-Operative, known locally as the Co-Op or just simply 'Co', was a major department store in Belfast.

Craic: news (usually of a humorous or entertaining nature).

Crater: someone perceived as not having had a lot of fortune.

Crumlin Road / King's Hall / Royal Avenue: well-known places in Belfast.

Cute hoor: a sly person.

Dead beat: *extremely tired / thoroughly exhausted.*

Eejit: *someone silly, without common sense.*

Fluthered: *drunk.*

Glentaisie and Glenaan: *two of the famous Nine Glens of Antrim.*

Guldered: *shouted.*

Gulpin: *a silly person (similar to 'eejit').*

Hames: *a mess.*

Kupala: *a festival in Poland (and other East European countries), part of which involves a young woman casting a floral wreath into the river. It's said that, if a young man retrieves it, he is her true love.*

Maine: *a river in Northern Ireland.*

Mater: *The Mater Infirmorum, a Belfast hospital. The correct pronunciation of 'Mater' rhymes with 'patter' but it is commonly mispronounced to rhyme with 'later', as is the case in the poem.*

Nixer: *an extra job, the income from which isn't declared for tax purposes.*

Now you're suckin' diesel: *Now you've got it! You understand!*

Pale: *Historically, the area of Ireland, containing Dublin, under the control of the English Government in the late Middle Ages.*

Polis: *Local dialect for 'police'.*

Shebeen: *a place without a licence where drinks are sold.*

Sheugh: *(pronounced 'shuck'): a ditch.*

Spin you no guff: *tell you a load of nonsense / I'll tell you this straight.*

Standard Ten: *a model of car in the 1960s.*

Thran: *contrary, stubborn.*

Tuppence: *'Two pence' – a reference to pre-decimal currency in Northern Ireland. A very small amount of money.*

Wee gander: *a look around.*

Wheen: *a lot.*

Wianki: *(translated 'wreaths' in English) is the name associated with an annual cultural event in Krakow, Poland. (See Kupala, above).*

Wild difficult / wild dishevelled: *extremely difficult / very dishevelled.*

Wisla: *also known as the Vistula, it is Poland's longest river and flows through Krakow.*

Yins: *'Ones', e.g. 'My sheep are those yins (ones) over there.'*

Yon / thon: *that.*

Made in the USA
Charleston, SC
14 November 2016